Profitable

Forex

Strategies

Unlocking the Secrets of Currency Markets

George Andrew

Table of Contents

CHAPTER ONE

Introduction to Profitable Forex Strategies

The world of Forex trading, characterized by its dynamic nature and constant evolution, demands a strategic and informed approach to navigate the complexities of the financial markets. Profitable Forex strategies are at the core of successful trading, encompassing a diverse set of principles and techniques aimed at capitalizing on currency fluctuations while mitigating risks. As traders engage in the global foreign exchange market, understanding and implementing effective strategies become imperative for sustained success.

Profitable Forex strategies go beyond mere predictions of price movements; they involve a comprehensive understanding of market dynamics, risk management, and the ability to adapt to changing conditions. Whether one is a seasoned trader or a novice entering the realm of Forex, cultivating a well-thought-out strategy is paramount to achieving consistent profitability.

This exploration into profitable Forex strategies will delve into the fundamental components that contribute to successful trading. From risk management and technical analysis to advanced trading concepts and adapting to market changes, each facet plays a crucial role in formulating a strategy that not only maximizes gains but also safeguards against potential losses.

As we navigate through the intricacies of profitable Forex strategies, the goal is to provide a comprehensive overview, offering insights and practical guidance for traders at various stages of their journey. By delving into key concepts, advanced techniques, and real-world case studies, this exploration aims to equip traders with the knowledge and tools necessary to build, refine, and adapt their strategies, fostering resilience and success in the ever-evolving world of Forex trading.

Welcome to the captivating realm of "Profitable forex strategies" your passport to the thrilling world of currency trading. This book is not just a guide; it's your personal key to unlocking the potential for financial prosperity in the dynamic and ever-evolving Forex market.

Embark on a Journey of Financial Discovery

In the pages that follow, we invite you to join us on a journey that transcends borders, time zones, and traditional financial constraints. Forex trading isn't just a financial endeavor; it's a fascinating odyssey where every chart tells a story, and every trade is an opportunity to craft your financial destiny.

Navigate the Global Financial Seas with Confidence

Explore the vast landscape of the Forex market, where currencies ebb and flow like the tides of economic prosperity. From the bustling streets of Tokyo to the financial districts of New York, we demystify the intricacies of currency exchange, empowering you to navigate this global sea with confidence and savvy.

Craft Your Success: Strategies for Wealth Creation

But this book isn't just about understanding the market; it's about mastering it. We dive deep into the art and science of profitable trading strategies, unveiling the secrets of seasoned traders who have turned market volatility into their greatest ally. Learn not just how to trade but how to thrive in the world's largest financial arena.

Why "Profitable forex strategies" Is Your Ultimate Guide

Whether you're a seasoned trader or a curious beginner, "Profitable forex strategies" is designed to be your comprehensive companion. Packed with insights, strategies, and real-world examples, this book is not just about making profits; it's also about understanding the language of the market and using it to your advantage.

Get ready to embark on a transformative journey where financial possibilities are limitless, and the path to prosperity unfolds with every turn of the page. "Profitable forex strategies" — your gateway to mastering the art of currency wealth. Let the adventure begin.

Understanding the Forex Market

The foreign exchange market, often abbreviated as Forex or FX, stands as a global powerhouse, dictating the ebb and flow of currencies across borders. It's a decentralized market, meaning there is no physical location where trading occurs. Instead, it exists as a network of computers facilitating currency transactions 24 hours a day, five days a week.

1.1.1 Dynamics of Currency Trading

At the heart of the Forex market lies the fundamental concept of currency pairs. Currencies are traded in pairs, such as EUR/USD or GBP/JPY. Each pair represents the exchange rate between two currencies, reflecting the value of one currency in terms of the other. Traders engage in buying or selling currency pairs based on their expectations of how one currency will perform relative to the other.

1.1.2 Market Participants and Influences

The Forex market is a bustling arena with various participants influencing its dynamics. Major players include central banks, commercial banks, institutional investors, corporations, and individual traders. Central banks, for instance, play a crucial role by implementing monetary policies that impact currency values. Economic indicators, geopolitical events, and global economic trends are key factors that influence the market, making it a dynamic and complex environment.

1.1.3 Liquidity and Volatility

One of the market's defining characteristics is its high liquidity. The immense trading volume ensures that large transactions can be executed with minimal price impact. However, this liquidity also contributes to market volatility, creating opportunities for profit but also increasing risk. Traders must navigate this volatility by understanding market trends, utilizing technical analysis, and staying informed about economic events.

Importance of Profitable Strategies

1.2.1 Navigating Market Uncertainty

The Forex market's inherent unpredictability necessitates the adoption of well-defined and profitable trading strategies. Successful trading is not merely about luck; it is a systematic approach to understanding and capitalizing on market movements. Profitable strategies act as a compass, guiding traders through the intricate landscape of currency fluctuations.

1.2.2 Risk Management and Consistency

A cornerstone of profitable strategies lies in effective risk management. Traders must carefully assess and control their exposure to risk in each trade. This involves setting stop-loss orders, diversifying portfolios, and determining the appropriate position size. Consistency in applying these risk management principles is paramount for long-term success, protecting traders from significant losses and preserving their capital.

1.2.3 Technical and Fundamental Analysis

Profitable strategies often blend technical and fundamental analysis. Technical analysis involves studying price charts, patterns, and indicators to forecast future price movements. Fundamental analysis, on the other hand, considers economic indicators, central bank policies, and geopolitical events to understand the underlying factors affecting currency values. Combining these approaches enhances a trader's ability to make well-informed decisions.

1.2.4 Adapting to Market Conditions

The Forex market is dynamic, with conditions that can change rapidly. Profitable strategies are adaptable, allowing traders to adjust their approach based on market trends, volatility, and economic developments. This adaptability ensures that strategies remain effective in various market environments, from trending to range-bound conditions.

In conclusion, understanding the Forex market and employing profitable strategies are integral components of successful currency trading. Traders who grasp the intricacies of currency dynamics and develop sound strategies position themselves to navigate the complexities of the Forex market and capitalize on its vast opportunities.

CHAPTER TWO

2.0 Fundamentals of Profitable Forex Trading

2.1 Risk Management

Risk management is a cornerstone of successful Forex trading. It involves strategies and techniques aimed at minimizing potential losses and preserving capital. Traders often use the concept of risk-reward ratio, where they assess the potential profit against the potential loss for each trade. Setting stop-loss orders is a common practice to limit losses, ensuring that a trade is automatically closed if it reaches a predefined level of loss. Diversification, position sizing, and not risking too much capital on a single trade are essential components of effective risk management.

2.2 Market Analysis

Market analysis is crucial for making informed trading decisions. There are two primary types of analysis: fundamental and technical. Fundamental analysis involves evaluating economic indicators, geopolitical events, and other macroeconomic factors that can influence currency prices. Economic indicators such as GDP growth, interest rates, and employment figures are closely monitored. Technical analysis, on the other hand, involves studying historical price charts and using various indicators to identify trends and potential entry and exit points. A combination of both approaches is often employed for a comprehensive understanding of market conditions.

2.3 Trading Psychology

The psychological aspect of trading is often underestimated but plays a pivotal role in a trader's success. Emotions such as fear, greed, and impatience can lead to irrational decision-making and poor trading outcomes. Successful traders cultivate discipline and emotional control. They adhere to a well-defined trading plan, sticking to predetermined entry and exit points. Accepting losses as a part of trading and not letting past successes or failures impact future decisions is essential. Continuous learning, self-awareness, and the ability to adapt to changing market conditions contribute to a trader's psychological resilience.

In summary, mastering the fundamentals of profitable Forex trading requires a holistic approach. Rigorous risk management, a sound understanding of market analysis techniques, and disciplined trading psychology are interconnected elements that, when combined, form the foundation for sustainable success in the dynamic and challenging world of Forex trading.

CHAPTER THREE

3. Technical Analysis Techniques

3.1 Candlestick Patterns

Candlestick patterns are a vital component of technical analysis, offering insights into price movements and market sentiment. Each candlestick represents a specific time period, and the patterns formed by these candles help traders predict potential price reversals or continuations. Common patterns include doji, engulfing, and hammer. Doji signals indecision in the market, while engulfing patterns suggest a potential reversal. The hammer pattern often indicates a reversal after a downtrend. Traders use these patterns in combination with other indicators to make more informed decisions about market entry and exit points.

3.2 Trend Analysis

Trend analysis is fundamental to understanding the direction of price movements. Traders identify trends by analyzing price charts over different time frames. Trends can be upward (bullish), downward (bearish), or sideways (range-bound). Various technical tools, such as trendlines, moving averages, and trend indicators like the Moving Average Convergence Divergence (MACD), assist in recognizing and confirming trends. Trend analysis helps traders align their trades with the prevailing market direction, increasing the likelihood of profitable outcomes.

3.3 Support and Resistance

Support and resistance levels are critical concepts in technical analysis. Support is a price level at which a currency pair or asset tends to stop falling and may bounce back upwards. Resistance, conversely, is a price level where upward movement may stall or reverse. These levels are identified by historical price data and play a crucial role in decision-making. Traders often use them to set entry and exit points, as well as stop-loss orders. Breakouts above resistance or below support can signal potential trend changes, adding valuable information to a trader's analysis.

In conclusion, technical analysis techniques are powerful tools that provide traders with a systematic approach to understanding and predicting market movements. Candlestick patterns offer insights into market sentiment, trend analysis helps identify the overall direction, and support and resistance levels guide decision-making by highlighting key price levels. Successful traders often integrate these techniques into a comprehensive strategy, combining technical analysis with other fundamental and risk management principles for a well-rounded approach to trading.

CHAPTER FOUR

4.0 Fundamental Analysis in Forex

4.1 Economic Indicators

Economic indicators are crucial components of fundamental analysis in the Forex market. These indicators provide insights into the economic health of a country and, consequently, influence the value of its currency. Key indicators include Gross Domestic Product (GDP), inflation rates, employment figures, and consumer confidence. Traders closely monitor these indicators as they can impact currency values and provide signals about the overall health and stability of an economy. For example, a robust GDP growth may strengthen a country's currency, while high inflation could weaken it.

4.2 Central Bank Policies

Central bank policies play a pivotal role in fundamental analysis. Central banks, such as the Federal Reserve in the United States or the European Central Bank, set interest rates and implement monetary policies that directly influence currency values. Traders pay close attention to central bank statements, interest rate decisions, and policy outlooks. A central bank signaling potential interest rate hikes may attract foreign capital, strengthening the currency. Conversely, indications of economic challenges or lower interest rates can lead to a currency depreciation.

4.3 News Trading Strategies

News trading involves capitalizing on market movements triggered by significant economic events and announcements. Traders utilizing news trading strategies closely follow economic calendars and news releases, focusing on events that can cause volatility in the Forex market. Popular news events include interest rate decisions, employment reports, and geopolitical developments. Traders often prepare for such events by placing orders with specified entry and exit points to take advantage of rapid price movements. However, news trading requires caution due to the inherent unpredictability and potential for market whipsaws.

In summary, fundamental analysis in Forex encompasses a thorough understanding of economic indicators, central bank policies, and the implementation of news trading strategies. Economic indicators provide insights into a country's economic health, central bank policies directly influence currency values, and news trading strategies allow traders to capitalize on short-term market movements triggered by significant events. Successful Forex traders often combine fundamental analysis with technical analysis and risk management strategies to form a comprehensive and well-informed trading approach.

CHAPTER FIVE

5.0 Popular Forex Trading Strategies

5.1 Day Trading Strategies

Day trading is a Forex trading strategy where positions are opened and closed within the same trading day. Traders engaging in day trading aim to capitalize on short-term price movements, often utilizing technical analysis and intraday chart patterns. Common day trading strategies include scalping, where traders seek small price fluctuations for quick profits, and momentum trading, where positions are taken based on the continuation of existing trends. Day traders must stay well-informed about market conditions, economic events, and technical indicators, as decisions are made swiftly within the context of a single trading day.

5.2 Swing Trading Strategies

Swing trading is a strategy that aims to capture price "swings" or trends over a period of days to weeks. Traders employing swing trading strategies typically use a combination of technical and fundamental analysis to identify potential entry and exit points. This approach allows for a more relaxed trading pace compared to day trading, as positions are held for a more extended period. Key elements of swing trading include trend identification, support and resistance analysis, and the use of technical indicators to confirm potential trend reversals or continuations.

5.3 Position Trading Strategies

Position trading is a longer-term Forex trading strategy where traders hold positions for weeks, months, or even years. This strategy is often based on fundamental analysis, taking into account economic indicators, central bank policies, and other macroeconomic factors. Position traders aim to capitalize on major market trends, avoiding the noise and short-term fluctuations that may occur in the market. Successful position trading requires a patient and disciplined approach, as traders need to withstand market volatility and have a broader perspective on the economic fundamentals driving currency movements.

In conclusion, popular Forex trading strategies cater to various trading styles and timeframes. Day trading focuses on short-term price movements within a single day, swing trading aims to capture trends over days to weeks, and position trading adopts a longer-term perspective, leveraging fundamental analysis to identify major market trends. Traders often choose a strategy that aligns with their risk tolerance, time commitment, and market analysis preferences, while also considering the unique characteristics of the Forex market.

CHAPTER SIX

6.0 Building Your Profitable Forex Strategy

6.1 Customizing Strategies to Your Risk Tolerance

Building a profitable Forex strategy begins with understanding and customizing it to your risk tolerance. Assessing how much risk you are comfortable with per trade and overall in your portfolio is crucial. Different trading strategies come with varying levels of risk, and aligning your strategy with your risk tolerance helps ensure emotional stability during market fluctuations. This involves setting appropriate stop-loss orders, determining position sizes, and avoiding over-leveraging. A well-customized strategy allows you to stay disciplined and focused on long-term success.

6.2 Combining Technical and Fundamental Analysis

A robust Forex strategy often involves a combination of technical and fundamental analysis. Technical analysis helps identify trends, entry and exit points, and potential reversals using historical price data and chart patterns. On the other hand, fundamental analysis considers economic indicators, central bank policies, and geopolitical events to understand the broader market context. By combining these approaches, traders can benefit from a comprehensive understanding of the market, making more informed and well-rounded decisions. The synergy of technical and fundamental analysis enhances the overall effectiveness of a trading strategy.

6.3 Backtesting and Optimization

Backtesting and optimization are critical steps in building a profitable Forex strategy. Backtesting involves applying your strategy to historical market data to assess its performance. This process helps identify strengths and weaknesses, allowing for adjustments before risking real capital.

Optimization involves fine-tuning your strategy based on backtesting results, considering factors like changing market conditions. However, it's essential to strike a balance – over-optimization can lead to a strategy that performs well historically but fails in real-time trading. Regularly reviewing and adapting your strategy based on market dynamics is key to its ongoing success.

In summary, building a profitable Forex strategy is a dynamic process that involves customization to your risk tolerance, combining technical and fundamental analysis for a comprehensive view, and rigorously backtesting and optimizing your approach. Successful strategies are not static but evolve over time, adapting to changing market conditions and incorporating lessons learned from both successes and setbacks. Developing and refining your strategy is a continuous journey that requires discipline, adaptability, and a commitment to ongoing learning and improvement.

CHAPTER SEVEN

7.0 Advanced Trading Concepts

7.1 Fibonacci Retracement and Extension

Fibonacci retracement and extension are advanced technical analysis tools widely used in Forex trading. Derived from the Fibonacci sequence, these levels help identify potential reversal or extension points in price movements. Traders use retracement levels (38.2%, 50%, 61.8%) to identify potential support or resistance areas during a pullback. Extension levels (127.2%, 161.8%) are utilized to project potential price targets in the direction of the prevailing trend. Integrating Fibonacci analysis into a trading strategy requires a keen understanding of price dynamics and the ability to identify key Fibonacci levels for more precise entry and exit points.

7.2 Trading Divergences

Trading divergences involves analyzing discrepancies between price movements and technical indicators, signaling potential changes in market direction. Bullish divergence occurs when prices make lower lows, but the indicator makes higher lows, suggesting a potential upward reversal. Conversely, bearish divergence occurs when prices make higher highs, but the indicator makes lower highs, indicating a potential downward reversal. Trading divergences requires a deep understanding of market momentum and the chosen indicators, such as the Relative Strength Index (RSI) or Moving Average Convergence

Divergence (MACD), to identify divergence signals accurately.

7.3 Algorithmic Trading

Algorithmic trading, or algo trading, is the use of computer algorithms to execute trading strategies automatically. This advanced concept leverages pre-programmed instructions to analyze market conditions and execute trades with speed and precision. Algo trading can be based on various factors, including technical indicators, statistical models, or even news sentiment analysis. This approach eliminates emotional decision-making, ensures quick execution, and allows for backtesting and optimization. However, implementing algorithmic trading requires programming skills, a solid understanding of market dynamics, and continuous monitoring to adapt to changing conditions.

In conclusion, advanced trading concepts like Fibonacci retracement, trading divergences, and algorithmic trading add depth and sophistication to a trader's toolkit. Incorporating these concepts into a trading strategy demands a higher level of skill, experience, and a nuanced understanding of market behavior. While these concepts offer powerful insights and automation capabilities, it's essential for traders to approach them with a thorough understanding of their principles and potential limitations, ensuring a balanced and informed application in the dynamic and complex world of Forex trading.

CHAPTER EIGHT

8.0 Case Studies: Successful Forex Traders

8.1 Learning from Successful Traders

Studying successful Forex traders provides valuable insights into the strategies, mindset, and practices that contribute to their success. One common trait among successful traders is a commitment to continuous learning. They stay informed about market trends, economic indicators, and evolving trading techniques. Successful traders often emphasize the importance of discipline, risk management, and the ability to adapt to changing market conditions. Learning from their experiences helps aspiring traders refine their own strategies, avoid common pitfalls, and build a solid foundation for navigating the complexities of the Forex market.

8.2 Real-world Application of Strategies

Case studies of successful Forex traders offer practical examples of how various strategies are applied in real-world scenarios. Whether it's day trading, swing trading, or position trading, these case studies showcase how traders analyze market conditions, identify entry and exit points, and manage risk. Additionally, they highlight the importance of combining technical and fundamental analysis, as well as the integration of advanced concepts like Fibonacci retracement and algorithmic trading. Real-world applications provide a bridge between theoretical knowledge and practical execution, allowing traders to see how successful individuals navigate the dynamic and unpredictable nature of the Forex market.

Studying successful traders also emphasizes the significance of emotional resilience and the ability to learn from failures. Many successful traders have experienced setbacks but used those experiences as learning opportunities. This resilience, combined with a commitment to self-improvement, contributes to their long-term success. Aspiring traders can draw inspiration from these case studies, incorporating the lessons learned into their own trading strategies and approaches.

- In conclusion, case studies of successful Forex traders serve as invaluable educational resources. By learning from their experiences, traders can gain practical insights, refine their strategies, and develop the mental discipline required for success in the challenging world of Forex trading. These case studies bridge the gap between theory and practice, offering a nuanced understanding of how successful traders navigate the complexities of the market, manage risk, and continually evolve to stay ahead in a dynamic financial landscape.

CHAPTER NINE

9.0 Risk Mitigation and Money Management

9.1 Importance of Proper Position Sizing

Proper position sizing is a fundamental aspect of effective risk mitigation and money management in Forex trading. It involves determining the amount of capital to risk on each trade to protect the overall trading account from significant losses. Traders often use a percentage-based approach, risking a small portion of their capital on each trade. This ensures that a series of losing trades does not deplete the trading account entirely. By implementing proper position sizing, traders can maintain consistency and longevity in their trading careers, safeguarding against the impact of unforeseen market movements.

9.2 Diversification Strategies

Diversification is a key strategy for risk mitigation in Forex trading. Instead of concentrating capital on a single currency pair, traders spread their investments across different assets or currency pairs. This helps reduce the impact of poor performance in one position on the overall portfolio. Diversification can be achieved through trading various currency pairs, incorporating different trading strategies, or even diversifying into other asset classes. While diversification does not eliminate risk entirely, it provides a risk reduction mechanism, enhancing the resilience of a trading portfolio against adverse market conditions.

9.3 Contingency Planning

Contingency planning involves preparing for unexpected events and adverse market conditions. This includes having a clear risk management plan, setting stop-loss orders, and defining exit strategies in advance. Traders should also be aware of potential market-moving events, such as economic releases or geopolitical developments, and be prepared to adjust their positions accordingly. Having a well-defined contingency plan helps traders make informed decisions under pressure, reducing the impact of emotional reactions to unforeseen circumstances. Additionally, traders may use risk management tools like options or hedging strategies to further protect their positions in the face of uncertainty.

In summary, risk mitigation and money management are integral components of successful Forex trading. Proper position sizing ensures the preservation of capital, diversification strategies spread risk across different assets, and contingency planning equips traders to navigate unforeseen market events. By incorporating these elements into their trading approach, traders can foster a resilient and sustainable trading environment, enhancing their ability to weather challenges and achieve long-term success in the dynamic world of Forex.

CHAPTER TEN

10.0 Adapting to Market Changes

10.1 Recognizing Market Trends

Adapting to market changes begins with the ability to recognize evolving trends. Market trends can be upward (bullish), downward (bearish), or sideways (range-bound). Traders use technical analysis tools such as trendlines, moving averages, and trend indicators to identify and confirm trends. Recognizing market trends is crucial for aligning trading strategies with the prevailing market direction. By staying attuned to changing trends, traders can adjust their positions, entry and exit points, and overall strategy to capitalize on emerging opportunities while mitigating potential risks.

10.2 Adjusting Strategies in Volatile Markets

Volatility is a constant factor in the Forex market, and adapting to it is essential for sustained success.

In highly volatile markets, traditional strategies may need adjustments to accommodate rapid price movements. Traders might opt for wider stop-loss orders, reduce position sizes, or utilize more conservative leverage. Additionally, adopting strategies like range trading or employing options to hedge positions can be effective in volatile conditions. Flexibility and the ability to adjust strategies based on market volatility are crucial for navigating unpredictable market movements and ensuring resilience in the face of changing conditions.

10.3 Staying Informed About Global Events

Staying informed about global events is a cornerstone of adapting to market changes. Economic releases, geopolitical developments, and central bank announcements can significantly impact currency values. Traders need to be aware of scheduled events and breaking news that may influence the Forex market. This information allows for proactive adjustments to positions and risk management strategies. A comprehensive understanding of how global events may affect currency pairs helps traders anticipate potential market shifts, enabling them to make timely and informed decisions in response to changing economic and geopolitical landscapes.

In conclusion, adapting to market changes is a dynamic process that involves recognizing trends, adjusting strategies in volatile conditions, and staying informed about global events. Successful traders are not rigid in their approaches but demonstrate the flexibility to modify their strategies based on evolving market dynamics. By incorporating these adaptive practices, traders enhance their ability to navigate the complexities of the Forex market, ensuring resilience and increasing the likelihood of long-term success.

CHAPTER ELEVEN

11. Conclusion

11.1 Recap of Key Strategies

In conclusion, successful Forex trading demands a strategic and disciplined approach. Key strategies include a robust risk management plan, incorporating proper position sizing and diversification to protect capital. A combination of technical and fundamental analysis provides a comprehensive understanding of market conditions, while advanced concepts like Fibonacci retracement and algorithmic trading offer additional tools for analysis. Real-world case studies of successful traders illustrate the practical application of these strategies, emphasizing the importance of adaptability and contingency planning in the face of market changes. Building a profitable Forex strategy involves a continuous learning process, integrating insights from successful traders and refining approaches through backtesting and optimization.

11.2 Continuous Learning and Improvement

The journey of Forex trading is marked by continuous learning and improvement. Markets evolve, and successful traders adapt to these changes. Embracing a mindset of continuous learning involves staying informed about economic indicators, global events, and emerging market trends. Traders should be open to exploring new strategies, refining existing ones, and incorporating lessons learned from both successes and failures. The commitment to improvement includes staying updated on technological advancements, algorithmic trading tools, and incorporating the latest insights from the ever-changing financial landscape. In the dynamic world of Forex, a dedication to continuous learning is the key to staying ahead of the curve and achieving sustained success.

In summary, Forex trading is a multifaceted endeavor that requires a combination of technical skills, strategic thinking, and a disciplined mindset. By implementing key strategies, learning from successful traders, and embracing a mindset of continuous improvement, traders can navigate the complexities of the Forex market, adapt to changing conditions, and position themselves for long-term success.

Anticipate new publications on this. Thanks

61